The Grasping Void

The Grasping Void

Matthew Petchinsky

The Grasping Void: Why You'll Regret This Purchase
By: Matthew Petchinsky

Introduction: *The Reluctant Reader's Guide*

Welcome, reluctant reader. Let me start by saying this: I don't know why you're here, and neither do you. Yet, against all logic and reason, you've picked up *The Grasping Void* and are now flipping through these pages, possibly expecting something—anything—to justify the decision you've made. Spoiler alert: you won't find it. This book has no reason to exist, and you, by extension, have no reason to be reading it. And yet, here we are, entwined in this strange, cosmic dance of futility. Fascinating, isn't it?

The truth is, this book is not about you, your aspirations, or your curiosities. It doesn't aim to educate, entertain, or inspire. It doesn't offer life-changing revelations or serve as an escape from the mundane. In fact, it is as mundane as a book can be. It's the literary equivalent of staring at a beige wall for hours and convincing yourself it's art. Why, then, does this book exist? The answer is as simple as it is perplexing: because it can.

Humans have an odd compulsion to engage with things they don't understand. You might not have wanted this book, but you felt compelled to own it, to hold it, to explore its inexplicable pull. Perhaps it's the same force that makes us press buttons marked "Do Not Touch" or peer into the dark corners of basements we'd rather avoid. Some books promise answers. This one promises nothing, yet here you are, flipping pages, expecting something—anything—to make sense.

Let me make it abundantly clear: this book does not care if you like it. It does not aim to be memorable, useful, or even coherent. It's not here to change your life, broaden your horizons, or spark meaningful conversation at your next book club meeting. *The Grasping Void* exists in a realm of self-aware absurdity, a monument to nothingness. You've stumbled into a paradox—a book that thrives on its lack of purpose.

And yet, the joke, if there is one, is on all of us. You're holding it. I wrote it. And between the two of us, we've created something that defies logic: a book that is as unremarkable as it is irresistible. Perhaps that's the magic of it—its sheer audacity to exist at all.

So, dear reader, I invite you to proceed, not because you'll gain anything from the pages ahead, but because you've already come this far. This is the journey you didn't know you were taking, the purchase you can't fully explain, and the experience you won't be able to describe to anyone else without a shrug and a shake of your head.

Welcome to the void. Let's grasp it together.

Chapter 1: *The Endless Spiral of Pointlessness*

It begins, as all things do, with a question. Why? Why did you pick up this book? Why are you reading it? Why do you even care about finding answers to these questions? These are the "whys" that form the nucleus of the human experience. Unfortunately, they are also the foundation of an infinite loop—a never-ending spiral of pointlessness that consumes time, energy, and often, sanity.

If you've ever stared into the night sky and wondered about your place in the universe, you've already stepped into the spiral. The stars don't answer back. They don't care. They just burn, indifferent to your gaze, your existence, or your search for meaning. And yet, there you were, looking for something—anything—that might make sense of it all. The irony is profound: the more we seek meaning, the more we realize how utterly devoid of meaning everything seems to be. This book is no different. Its existence is an absurd testament to the human condition, a mirror reflecting our endless quest for purpose in a void that has none.

Let's confront the reality of this spiral together. Think about the sheer futility of what you're doing right now. You're reading a book that openly declares it has no reason to exist, yet here you are, turning the pages. Somewhere in the back of your mind, you might hope that this chapter will veer into a deeper insight, a clever twist, or some profound revelation. But let me save you the trouble: it won't. The point of this chapter—and indeed, the entire book—is that there is no point. And that's the point.

This spiral, this endless loop of searching for meaning where there is none, is a microcosm of life itself. We wake up, eat, work, and sleep, only to repeat the process again and again, clinging to the hope that all this effort leads somewhere worthwhile. But does it? Or are we simply perpetuating the same cycle, pretending there's a destination at the end of the path because the alternative—that there isn't—feels unbearable?

Consider this: if you were told, definitively, that there is no grand purpose to life, would anything change? Would you stop eating? Stop working? Stop dreaming? Probably not. The spiral is insidious because even when confronted with its futility, we can't help but keep spinning. It's baked into our DNA, a survival mechanism that keeps us moving forward even when the destination is shrouded in uncertainty.

This chapter isn't here to offer solutions or to lift you out of the spiral. Instead, it's here to walk you deeper into it. Because, paradoxically, the only way to confront the absurdity of existence is to embrace it fully. Why are you reading this book? Why am I writing it? The answer doesn't matter. What matters is that we're here, spiraling together, creating meaning out of meaninglessness, if only for a fleeting moment.

There's a certain comfort in realizing that the spiral never ends. It liberates us from the pressure to find ultimate answers. If life is an endless loop, then perhaps the only thing left to do is laugh at its absurdity. And maybe, just maybe, that laughter is the closest thing we'll ever get to meaning.

So, dear reader, I invite you to continue spiraling with me. Turn the page. Read the next chapter. Not because it will lead you to some great epiphany, but because there's nothing else to do. Welcome to the spiral. You're already in it. Why not keep going?

Chapter 2: *Why Everything is Overrated*

Let's begin with the obvious: everything you've ever been told to love is overrated. From the gentle hues of a sunset to the wagging tail of an excitable puppy, the world is brimming with clichés that we collectively overvalue. It's not your fault, of course. Society has conditioned you to believe in the inherent worth of these things, layering them with so much sentimental fluff that it's nearly impossible to see them for what they truly are: profoundly ordinary.

Take sunsets, for instance. We're told they're magical, romantic, and awe-inspiring. Social media overflows with filtered photographs of sunsets captioned with insipid reflections like, "Lost in the colors of the sky." But let's strip away the sentimentality and look at the facts. A sunset is merely the Earth rotating on its axis, causing the sun's light to scatter through the atmosphere. The colors? A result of particles in the air refracting light waves. That's it. No magic, no romance—just basic physics at work. Yet, we gather on beaches, gaze wistfully at horizons, and attribute profound meaning to something that happens every single day without fail. Sunsets aren't unique. They're not even rare. They're just a predictable byproduct of the planet's rotation.

Now let's turn our attention to puppies. Who doesn't love a puppy, right? They're small, fluffy, and full of energy. But if we're being honest, they're also loud, messy, and a significant time investment. Every wag of their tail comes with a price: chewed shoes, midnight accidents on the carpet, and the incessant barking at shadows. Society tells us puppies symbolize innocence and joy, but in reality, they're high-maintenance creatures that demand constant attention. And for what? The fleeting satisfaction of a cuddle or a lick on the face, both of which are far less profound than we pretend they are. Puppies, like sunsets, are another overrated indulgence—a product of our collective tendency to romanti-cize the mundane.

The problem, of course, is not with sunsets or puppies themselves. They didn't ask for this level of adoration. The problem is with us. We elevate these things to near-mythical status because we're desperate for meaning, for beauty, for something to distract us from the otherwise re-lentless monotony of existence. It's easier to gush over a vibrant sky or a wagging tail than to confront the empty void within ourselves. And so, we ascribe value where none inherently exists, convincing ourselves that these trivialities are somehow essential to the human experience.

Consider other so-called "universally loved" things: warm hugs, rainy afternoons, a perfectly brewed cup of coffee. Strip them of their poetic framing, and what do you have? Hugs are merely two bodies pressing together—a primal act of shared body heat. Rainy afternoons are inconvenient, often causing traffic jams and soggy shoes. And coffee? A bitter liquid we've trained ourselves to crave for its ability to make mornings tolerable. These things aren't inherently wonderful. They're just things, imbued with significance only because we've been told they should matter.

It's not that these elements of life are inherently bad. They're just or-dinary. The issue lies in the cultural obsession with elevating them to something extraordinary, perpetuating the myth that they hold the key to happiness or fulfillment. In doing so, we set ourselves up for disap-pointment when the reality doesn't match the hype. The sunset fades, the puppy grows into a dog, and the coffee gets cold. What then? We're left chasing the next overrated experience, hoping it will finally live up to its reputation.

So, why do we do it? Why do we continue to overrate the mundane? The answer, as always, lies in the human need for distraction. By focus-ing on the supposed beauty of a sunset or the charm of a puppy, we can momentarily forget the overarching futility of it all. And perhaps that's the most overrated thing of all: the idea that these small pleasures can somehow make life bearable.

In the end, sunsets are just light, puppies are just animals, and everything you've ever been told to cherish is, in fact, overrated. But take heart, dear reader. Recognizing the mediocrity of these things is freeing. Once you strip away the illusions, you can see the world for what it truly is: a deeply ordinary place, filled with deeply ordinary things. And maybe—just maybe—that's okay. Or maybe it's not. Either way, the sunset will still set, and the puppy will still bark, entirely indifferent to what you think of them.

Chapter 3: *How to Waste Time Efficiently*

Time is often described as our most precious resource. Entire industries are built around the promise of helping us save it, manage it, and maximize its use. But what if, instead of chasing the illusion of productivity, we leaned into inefficiency? What if we mastered the art of wasting time? In this chapter, we'll explore the tools, techniques, and mindsets necessary to transform aimless dawdling into a finely honed craft.

Step 1: Overthinking Every Decision

One of the most effective ways to waste time is to overanalyze even the smallest choices. Want to order lunch? Spend 30 minutes scrolling through menus online, reading reviews, and agonizing over whether you should try that new sandwich shop or stick with your usual spot. For added inefficiency, write out a pros-and-cons list. By the time you've made your decision, you'll have successfully wasted a significant portion of your day on an activity that could have taken 30 seconds.

Step 2: The Endless Scroll

Modern technology offers an abundance of opportunities for efficient time-wasting, and the endless scroll is king among them. Social media platforms are designed to keep you glued to your screen, presenting an infinite stream of content you neither need nor truly enjoy. Lean into it. Start by opening your favorite app, then let the algorithm guide you. Watch pointless videos, read drama-filled comment threads, and follow links to articles you'll never finish. Bonus points if you convince yourself that you're "staying informed" or "connecting with others" while doing so.

Step 3: Start Projects You'll Never Finish

Embarking on a new project is a classic time-wasting strategy. Choose something ambitious, like learning a new language or building a ship in a bottle, but ensure you have no intention of following through. Spend hours researching materials, watching tutorials, and buying supplies you'll never use. The key here is to convince yourself that you're being productive while simultaneously making no real progress.

Step 4: Perfect the Art of Procrastination

Procrastination is often viewed as a negative habit, but in the context of wasting time efficiently, it's an essential skill. Begin by creating a to-do list filled with tasks you have no desire to complete. Then, spend hours reorganizing the list, color-coding priorities, and creating elaborate schedules for when you *might* tackle these tasks. When the time comes to actually work, find a reason to delay—whether it's cleaning your desk, checking emails, or deciding you simply need "one more coffee" before starting.

Step 5: Engage in Unproductive Conversations

Conversation is a wonderful way to kill time, especially when it serves no meaningful purpose. Call a friend or co-worker and steer the discussion toward trivial topics. Discuss the weather in excruciating detail, recount minor inconveniences from your day, or dive into gossip about people neither of you truly care about. The longer you can keep the conversation going without arriving at any meaningful conclusion, the more efficiently you've wasted time.

Step 6: Create Arbitrary Obstacles

If you want to waste time like a pro, learn to complicate simple tasks unnecessarily. For example, instead of writing an email in one sitting, draft it, revise it, and then spend hours debating the tone of a single sentence. Alternatively, when cooking dinner, insist on using a recipe that requires ingredients you don't have, forcing yourself to make an unnecessary trip to the store. By adding unnecessary steps to otherwise straightforward tasks, you can stretch them out indefinitely.

Step 7: Become a Perfectionist

Perfectionism is a powerful time-wasting tool. Insist on perfecting tasks that don't matter, like aligning every icon on your desktop or rearranging your bookshelf by color, genre, and height. Remember, the goal isn't to accomplish anything meaningful—it's to devote as much time as possible to irrelevant details. The more effort you put into achieving an unnecessary level of precision, the less time you'll have for anything else.

Step 8: Dive Into Rabbit Holes

The internet is a goldmine for rabbit holes. Start with a simple Google search for "how to tie a tie" and, an hour later, find yourself deep in an article about the history of neckwear in the Victorian era. Rabbit holes are particularly effective because they feel productive—you're learning something, after all!—even though the knowledge is entirely irrelevant to your life.

Step 9: Multitask Poorly

Contrary to popular belief, multitasking doesn't make you more efficient—it makes you slower and less focused. To maximize inefficiency, juggle multiple tasks simultaneously, ensuring none of them are completed effectively. For instance, try answering emails while watching a TV show and preparing dinner. You'll end up burning the food, sending typo-filled emails, and missing key plot points, ensuring a complete waste of time across the board.

Step 10: Celebrate Your Inefficiency

Finally, the true hallmark of efficient time-wasting is embracing it wholeheartedly. Don't let guilt or shame cloud your efforts. Celebrate the hours spent achieving nothing. Post a picture of your perfectly aligned bookshelf or your half-finished craft project on social media with the caption, "Productive day!" By framing your inefficiency as intentional, you can turn time-wasting into an art form.

Conclusion

In a world obsessed with productivity, wasting time efficiently is a rebellious act. It's a way of reclaiming the hours you might otherwise spend chasing goals or meeting expectations. So go forth and waste time with purpose. Master the techniques outlined in this chapter, and you'll soon find yourself marveling at just how little you've accomplished—and enjoying every moment of it.

Chapter 4: *A Comprehensive History of Blank Pages*

The blank page is a curious anomaly in the world of literature, a space both full of potential and utterly devoid of content. Most readers barely register its presence, turning past it without a second thought, yet the blank page is an integral part of the book's anatomy. Its existence has sparked confusion, frustration, and, in rare cases, existential musings. Why is it there? What purpose does it serve? In this chapter, we delve into the long, absurd, and surprisingly detailed history of blank pages, exploring their origins, evolution, and persistent role in modern books.

The Dawn of Blank Pages: A Happy Accident

The story of blank pages begins not with intention, but with happenstance. In the early days of bookmaking, when texts were painstakingly hand-copied by monks in dimly lit scriptoria, blank pages often emerged as a byproduct of human error. A scribe, distracted by a stray thought or the monotony of the task, might accidentally skip a line, leaving an entire page blank to maintain the symmetry of the manuscript.

These early blank pages were not celebrated—they were seen as wasteful and careless. But over time, scribes began to use them to their advantage, adding notes, illustrations, or even prayers to fill the space. The blank page, once a mistake, became a canvas for creativity, setting the stage for its eventual formalization.

The Printing Press Era: Blank Pages Take Shape

The advent of the printing press in the 15th century brought efficiency to book production but also introduced new challenges. Unlike hand-copied manuscripts, printed books were constrained by the rigid structure of printing plates and signatures (groups of pages printed together). These signatures, often composed of multiples of four, eight, or sixteen pages, dictated the layout of the book. If a book's content didn't perfectly fill the number of pages in a signature, blank pages were left at the end to balance the layout.

For example, a text requiring 62 pages would necessitate a 64-page signature, leaving two pages blank. Rather than waste these pages, printers began to embrace them, using them for notes, errata, or advertisements. This practical necessity marked the first widespread use of blank pages as an intentional design element.

The Age of Enlightenment: Blank Pages as a Philosophical Statement

As books became more accessible during the Enlightenment, blank pages began to take on a new, more profound significance. Philosophers and authors, ever keen to imbue even the simplest things with meaning, saw the blank page as a metaphor for human potential. It was a space waiting to be filled, a silent invitation to readers to contribute their own thoughts or reflections.

Jean-Jacques Rousseau famously declared, "A blank page is the truest form of freedom," while Voltaire, in a moment of sardonic wit, described blank pages as "the only part of a book that cannot be misinterpreted."

This philosophical embrace of the blank page elevated it beyond mere practicality. It became a statement, a deliberate pause in the narrative, inviting contemplation.

The Victorian Era: Blank Pages as Social Tools

In the 19th century, the rise of the novel brought new uses for blank pages. Publishers began to leave blank pages at the front or back of books, encouraging readers to inscribe dedications, ownership notes, or even personal reflections. These pages transformed books into social artifacts, recording the lives and sentiments of their owners.

During this era, blank pages also became a marketing tool. Publishers used them to advertise other titles or subscription services, turning otherwise empty space into a profit-generating opportunity. This dual-purpose blank page—both personal and commercial—cemented its place in the bookmaking tradition.

The 20th Century: Blank Pages for Formatting and Aesthetics

By the 20th century, blank pages were no longer a matter of necessity but one of design. Publishers used them to create visual balance, separating sections or chapters with deliberate white space. Blank pages also served as buffers to protect delicate illustrations, ensuring they wouldn't smear or transfer ink onto the opposite page.

The blank page became a deliberate choice, an aesthetic tool to guide the reader's experience. Designers recognized its power to create rhythm and pace, using it as a pause in the flow of text, much like a rest in a musical composition.

Modern Times: The Persistent Mystery of the Blank Page

Today, blank pages persist in books for a variety of reasons. Some are functional, marking the end of a signature or providing space for readers to jot down notes. Others are purely decorative, a nod to tradition or an effort to maintain the visual harmony of a book.

Despite their ubiquity, blank pages remain a source of fascination. Why do we tolerate these seemingly wasted spaces? Perhaps it's because they offer a moment of silence in a noisy world, a rare pause that invites reflection. Or perhaps, as some theorists suggest, blank pages are a subtle psychological trick, making a book feel more substantial than it truly is.

The Future of Blank Pages: An Endangered Species?

As digital books rise in popularity, the blank page faces an uncertain future. E-books, unburdened by the constraints of printing signatures, have little need for blank space. Yet, even in the digital realm, echoes of the blank page persist—whether in the form of loading screens or intentional white space between sections.

The blank page, it seems, is as resilient as it is enigmatic. From its accidental origins to its philosophical and practical evolution, it has carved out a unique place in the history of books. And while its role may continue to change, one thing is certain: the blank page will always hold a curious fascination, inviting us to pause, reflect, and wonder why it's there at all.

Chapter 5: *The Secrets You Already Know*

The allure of hidden knowledge is universal. We crave the thrill of discovery, the satisfaction of unveiling secrets that promise to change our lives forever. Yet, many so-called secrets are not hidden at all. They are truths so glaringly obvious, so fundamentally ingrained in our daily lives, that we overlook them entirely. In this chapter, we will explore the "secrets" you already know—those nuggets of wisdom you didn't need a book, a seminar, or a guru to tell you.

Secret #1: You Need to Drink Water

This might come as a shock, but your body requires water to function. Dehydration leads to headaches, fatigue, and even death in extreme cases. Yet, countless self-help guides and wellness influencers frame drinking water as a revolutionary discovery. "Hydrate to thrive!" they proclaim, as if the importance of water hasn't been universally acknowledged since the dawn of humanity. The truth? You already knew this. You've known it since you first felt thirsty.

Secret #2: Exercise is Good for You

Let's break new ground here: moving your body is beneficial. Exercise improves your mood, strengthens your heart, and helps maintain a healthy weight. This is not groundbreaking information—it's been drilled into you since your first gym class. Yet, fitness gurus continue to market exercise as a life-altering secret. The only thing mysterious about exercise is why so many of us still avoid it, despite knowing its benefits.

Secret #3: Junk Food Isn't Great for Your Health

Do you really need someone to tell you that a steady diet of pizza, chips, and soda isn't the pinnacle of nutrition? The "secret" to a healthy lifestyle—eating more vegetables and less processed junk—is not hidden. It's right there, staring you in the face every time you opt for fries over a salad. The real mystery is why we keep hoping for some magical diet hack that lets us eat whatever we want without consequences.

Secret #4: Spending More Than You Earn Leads to Debt

Financial experts love to present this as groundbreaking wisdom: if you spend more money than you make, you'll go into debt. Shocking, isn't it? This "secret" is so obvious that even children understand it when they blow their allowance on candy and can't afford a new toy. Yet, entire industries profit from reminding us of this painfully self-evident truth.

Secret #5: Relationships Require Effort

Here's a revelation: maintaining healthy relationships takes work. Communication, compromise, and empathy are essential. If you neglect your partner, friends, or family, those relationships will deteriorate. This is not esoteric knowledge—it's basic human understanding. And yet, countless books, podcasts, and retreats promise to reveal the "hidden secrets" to a happy marriage or lasting friendships. Spoiler: you already know the answer. You just have to do the work.

Secret #6: Sleep is Important

The wellness industry has turned sleep into a multi-billion-dollar topic. Sleep trackers, apps, and bedtime routines are marketed as if the idea of getting enough rest is a revelation. But deep down, you already know the truth: when you don't sleep enough, you feel terrible. No amount of lavender-scented pillows or white noise machines will change the fundamental fact that you need 7–9 hours of sleep a night.

Secret #7: Procrastination Doesn't Help

Here's a groundbreaking insight: putting off important tasks doesn't make them go away. Procrastination only adds stress and leaves you scrambling at the last minute. Every student who's ever pulled an all-nighter or employee who's rushed to meet a deadline knows this. Yet, productivity gurus insist on treating this basic truth like it's an arcane piece of wisdom.

Secret #8: Complaining Without Action Changes Nothing

We all love a good venting session, but here's the deal: complaining without taking steps to fix the problem achieves nothing. It's cathartic, sure, but it doesn't change your situation. This isn't a hidden truth—it's something you know instinctively. Still, we indulge in grumbling as if it holds the key to transformation.

Secret #9: You Can't Please Everyone

No matter how hard you try, someone will always criticize you. This is not a secret. It's a fact of life. Yet, self-help books constantly remind us of this as if it's a profound realization. The reality is that we already know this truth—we just don't want to accept it.

Secret #10: Life is Unpredictable

Finally, the most obvious secret of all: life doesn't follow a script. Things happen unexpectedly. Plans fall apart. Opportunities arise out of nowhere. This is not a revelation—it's the nature of existence. The idea that anyone can teach you to control every aspect of your life is a comforting lie, but you've always known the truth: you can't predict the future.

Conclusion: The Truth Isn't Hidden

The "secrets" outlined in this chapter are not hidden gems of wisdom. They are truths so obvious that we often ignore them, seeking instead some magical insight that will transform our lives. But here's the real secret: the answers you're looking for are already within you. They always have been. The challenge isn't uncovering them—it's acting on them. And that, dear reader, is the only hidden truth worth knowing.

Chapter 6: *The Philosophy of Overthinking This Purchase*

The act of purchasing this book is, in itself, a fascinating philosophical conundrum. After all, the premise is clear: this is a book that declares, unapologetically, that it has no reason to exist. Its chapters are self-aware meditations on pointlessness, inefficiency, and absurdity. Yet, despite this—or perhaps because of it—you chose to buy it. Why? What psychological and philosophical processes led to this seemingly illogical decision? Let us explore, in painstaking detail, the layers of overthinking that likely unfolded in your mind before, during, and after the purchase.

Section 1: The Initial Encounter—Curiosity and Doubt

The journey begins with your first encounter with this book. Perhaps it was sitting on a shelf, its title intriguing yet nonsensical. Or maybe it was recommended by an algorithm that misread your preferences. Either way, you paused. A question flickered through your mind: *Why would anyone write a book like this?*

At this stage, your curiosity was piqued. The book's self-proclaimed lack of purpose created a paradox that demanded your attention. Surely, if the book is so openly pointless, it must also be something more—a clever satire, a hidden gem, or a cultural commentary. But what if it wasn't? What if it really was as pointless as it claimed? This doubt ignited the first spark of overthinking.

Section 2: The Rational Justification—"It's Justifiable, Right?"

Your next step was likely an attempt to rationalize the purchase. A part of you may have thought, *This could be funny. Maybe it's a critique of modern publishing, or a commentary on consumer culture.* You began constructing a narrative in which buying this book was not just a whimsical act but a meaningful decision.

At the same time, you likely evaluated the cost. Was it affordable? Perhaps you reasoned that even if the book turned out to be pointless, the financial loss would be negligible—a low-risk investment in curiosity. Or maybe you thought about the conversations this book could spark. *It'll be a conversation starter!* you might have told yourself, as if justifying the expenditure to some imaginary audience.

Section 3: The Existential Spiral—"What Does This Say About Me?"

As you lingered over the book, the decision became less about the book itself and more about you. What kind of person buys a book like this? Would purchasing it signify intellectual curiosity or gullibility? Would it reveal a sense of humor or an inability to resist clever marketing?

This existential spiral likely deepened as you considered your identity as a consumer. Was this book a reflection of your values, tastes, or personality? Were you, in fact, buying it to signal something to yourself or others? These questions, though fleeting, added another layer of complexity to your decision.

Section 4: The Social Element—"What Will Others Think?"

Human beings are social creatures, and even solitary decisions are rarely free from the influence of imagined judgment. You may have wondered how others would perceive your choice. Would friends think it was a waste of money? Would they see it as a quirky, ironic purchase?

Alternatively, you might have envisioned yourself explaining the book's premise to someone, hoping for a laugh or a nod of appreciation. The imagined reactions of others became part of the equation, subtly influencing your decision.

Section 5: The Sunk Cost of Decision-Making Time

By this point, you had likely spent several minutes contemplating whether to buy the book. This in itself became a factor. The more time you invested in the decision, the harder it became to walk away. After all, if you left without buying it, all that mental effort would have been wasted. This is known as the sunk cost fallacy, a cognitive bias that tricks us into justifying decisions based on previous investments rather than current value.

Section 6: The Final Push—Impulse and Irrationality

Ultimately, the decision to purchase this book was likely driven by impulse. Perhaps you thought, *Why not?* or *I have to know what this is about.* This final push transcended logic and reason, plunging you into the realm of irrationality. You didn't buy the book because it made sense—you bought it because *not* buying it felt like leaving an itch unscratched.

Section 7: Post-Purchase Rationalization—"It Was Worth It!"

After making the purchase, your mind likely shifted to justifying it. You may have thought, *Well, at least it's unique,* or *This will be fun to talk about.* Post-purchase rationalization is a common psychological phenomenon in which we convince ourselves that a decision was correct, even if doubts remain.

Interestingly, this rationalization loop continues as you read the book. Every chapter becomes an opportunity to reinforce your belief that the purchase was worthwhile—or to spiral further into self-reflection about why you made it in the first place.

Philosophical Implications: The Nature of Choice

Your decision to buy this book touches on profound philosophical questions about the nature of choice and desire. Did you choose this book, or did it choose you? Were you exercising free will, or were you influenced by external factors beyond your control? Is the act of purchasing something inherently tied to a search for meaning, even when the item itself declares its meaninglessness?

By overthinking this purchase, you've stumbled into an intellectual exercise that transcends the book itself. The simple act of buying it has become a metaphor for the human condition: a relentless quest to make sense of the absurd, to find purpose in the purposeless, and to justify our choices in an uncertain world.

Conclusion: The Beauty of Overthinking

In the end, your decision to buy this book wasn't about logic—it was about curiosity, identity, and the thrill of overthinking. And that's the beauty of it. This book may be pointless, but the thought process that led you here is anything but. It's a testament to the complexity of the human mind, capable of turning even the simplest decision into a philosophical journey. So, congratulations, dear reader. You've overthought your way into the pages of history—or at least into this absurdly self-aware book.

Chapter 7: *The Chapter That Should Have Been Left Out*

Ah, here we are, the proverbial black sheep of this literary family. The chapter that serves no purpose, contributes no value, and exists solely because it can. In a book filled with absurdities, this chapter dares to go one step further by defying even the pretense of coherence. Why does it exist? That's a question no one asked, and certainly one I have no intention of answering.

The Beginning of Nothingness

Let's start where most things do: the beginning. But what is a beginning, really? Is it a definitive moment of genesis, or is it simply an arbitrary point we've chosen to acknowledge? Consider, for instance, the concept of time. We measure it meticulously, yet it's nothing more than an endless stream of moments. Each second folds into the next, much like this chapter—unfolding without any clear direction.

Do you feel the weight of that yet? The slow, creeping realization that this might not go anywhere? Good. That's the intention. Or perhaps it isn't. Who's to say?

A Brief Detour Into Irrelevance

Let's pause to discuss something completely unrelated. Imagine a small bird perched on a windowsill. The bird, let's say, is a sparrow. It has feathers. Brown ones. Maybe a hint of gray. It chirps. What does it chirp about? We'll never know because birds don't speak our language, and frankly, they wouldn't care to even if they could. And yet, the bird remains there, a silent witness to your life, indifferent to your struggles or triumphs.

This bird has nothing to do with the chapter. But now that you've pictured it, it's part of your day, and you'll never get that moment back. Strange, isn't it?

The Longest Paragraph About Nothing

What if we wrote a paragraph that just kept going? Not for any specific reason, mind you, but simply because we could. A paragraph so meandering, so profoundly disconnected from anything resembling a coherent thought, that it leaves you questioning why you're still reading it. Imagine a sentence that begins with one topic but inexplicably shifts to another without warning, like a conversation with someone who's easily distracted. Perhaps we start by mentioning clouds—those fluffy accumulations of water vapor suspended in the sky—and then segue into a commentary on the existential dread one feels when realizing they forgot to thaw the chicken for dinner. Before you know it, we're discussing the peculiar way socks disappear in the laundry, which isn't really a mystery but more of a statistical inevitability, much like how this paragraph will eventually end, though not before you've lost a small but significant portion of your will to continue reading.

The Point Where It Could Have Stopped, But Didn't

By now, you're probably thinking, *Surely this chapter has run its course.* And yet, here we are, pressing forward into the unknown—or rather, the unneeded. But what if that's the point? What if the very existence of this chapter is a statement on the futility of seeking purpose where none exists? Or maybe that's giving it too much credit. Maybe it's just a waste of space.

Consider this: What if the act of reading this chapter is akin to eating a plain cracker? Not because you're hungry, but because it's there. It offers no flavor, no nutrition, and yet you keep chewing because stopping feels even more unsatisfying.

A Metaphor That Doesn't Quite Land

Let's explore a metaphor. Imagine this chapter as a cul-de-sac in a suburban neighborhood. You turn down the street, expecting it to lead somewhere, only to find yourself looping back to the main road. It's not a journey—it's an interruption, a brief detour that accomplishes nothing but forces you to turn your wheel. But even that metaphor fails to capture the true essence of this chapter because, unlike a cul-de-sac, it doesn't end neatly. It just keeps going, circling itself in increasingly tedious ways.

Words About Words

Here's an idea: let's talk about the words you're reading right now. These words are composed of letters, which are symbols representing sounds, which are themselves abstractions of meaning. But what is meaning, really? Is it something intrinsic to the words, or is it something you, the reader, impose upon them? In the context of this chapter, the answer is clear: there is no meaning. These words are empty vessels, drifting aimlessly in the sea of your attention span.

A Sudden and Unnecessary Anecdote

Once, there was a man who spent an entire day trying to balance a pencil on its eraser. He succeeded for a moment, but the pencil fell as soon as he turned away. This anecdote has no relevance to anything, but it occupies space on this page, much like this chapter occupies space in this book. You could argue that both the man and this chapter are exercises in futility, but even that comparison feels too generous.

The Inevitable Non-Conclusion

If you've made it this far, you're probably wondering how this chapter will end. The truth is, it won't. Not really. It will simply stop, leaving you to grapple with the fact that you've spent precious minutes of your life reading something that was designed to go nowhere.

And perhaps that's the most fitting conclusion of all: not a conclusion, but an abrupt cessation of words. A silence where something meaningful might have been.

Or maybe it's just the end.

Chapter 8: *The Unwritten Ending*

And now we come to the end, or at least, what we've arbitrarily decided to call "the end." But let's not fool ourselves: this book, like life itself, doesn't truly end—it just stops. No grand revelation, no satisfying conclusion, no moment of clarity to tie everything together. It began without purpose, meandered through chapters that defied coherence, and now it concludes in much the same way—except now, it's lighter in your hands, and your wallet is lighter too.

The Illusion of Closure

Endings are supposed to provide closure. They're meant to resolve conflicts, answer questions, and leave the audience with a sense of satisfaction. But what if there was nothing to resolve in the first place? This book offered no plot, no characters, no stakes. Its chapters were self-contained voids, united only by their shared refusal to deliver anything of substance. What, then, is there to close? How do you end something that never truly began?

This, dear reader, is the paradox of the unwritten ending. By its very nature, it refuses to end because it was never fully written. It doesn't tie up loose ends because there were no threads to begin with. It's a blank page masquerading as a conclusion, daring you to assign meaning to its absence of meaning.

The Transactional Truth

Let's address the elephant in the room: you paid for this. You willingly exchanged your money for a book that openly declared itself pointless. Perhaps you expected irony, wit, or some deeper commentary hidden beneath its absurd premise. Perhaps you believed that by the final chapter, it would all make sense. If that's the case, let me be clear: it doesn't.

But here's the beauty of it—you knew this all along. The back cover, the introduction, and every chapter leading up to this point told you exactly what to expect. You weren't deceived. You were complicit. This wasn't a scam; it was a transaction. You paid for the experience of holding this book, of turning its pages, of grappling with its unapologetic emptiness. And in return, you received exactly what was promised: nothing.

The Reader's Complicity

You might feel a twinge of regret now, or perhaps a sense of amusement. Either way, you're here, at the end, having completed a journey you didn't need to take. But let's not place all the blame on the book. You, dear reader, are just as responsible. You could have put it down at any moment. You could have returned it, ignored it, or chosen something else entirely. Yet, you didn't. You stayed. You read. You allowed yourself to be drawn into the absurdity of it all.

Why? Perhaps it was curiosity. Perhaps it was stubbornness. Or perhaps it was the hope that somewhere within these pages, you'd find a kernel of meaning. Whatever your reasons, they brought you here, to this unwritten ending.

The Reflection of Life Itself

In many ways, this book is a microcosm of life. We begin without understanding why, navigate a series of seemingly disconnected events, and eventually arrive at an ending that feels arbitrary and unresolved. We seek purpose, but purpose remains elusive. We spend time, energy, and resources chasing something—anything—that will make sense of it all. And in the end, all we're left with is the experience itself.

This book doesn't try to hide its pointlessness. It embraces it, flaunts it, even celebrates it. And by doing so, it holds up a mirror to the human condition, reminding us that sometimes, the journey is all there is. Not because the journey is meaningful, but because it's the only thing we have.

The Final Act of Defiance

So, what now? The pages ahead are blank, a silent acknowledgment that there is nothing left to say. This chapter doesn't end because it has resolved anything—it ends because it must. Books, like all things, require a stopping point, even if that point is arbitrary.

And yet, the ending of this book defies traditional notions of closure. It refuses to wrap things up neatly. It denies you the satisfaction of a conclusive takeaway. Instead, it leaves you with a question: *Why did I read this?*

The answer, of course, is yours to determine. Maybe you read it for the novelty. Maybe you read it out of sheer stubbornness. Or maybe you read it because you saw something of yourself in its absurdity.

The Real Conclusion: You Own It Now

The real ending of this book isn't on the final page—it's in your ownership of it. It sits on your shelf, a monument to your curiosity, your choices, and your willingness to embrace the absurd. It's a reminder that sometimes, we engage with things not because they're necessary or meaningful, but because they simply *are*.

And so, dear reader, as you close this book for the last time, remember: it ends as it began, with no purpose, no direction, and no reason to exist. Except, of course, that it does exist—and now, it exists with your money.

Congratulations. You've reached the unwritten ending. Or perhaps, it has reached you.

Appendix A: *Refund Policies You'll Never Use*

Let's face it: you're not returning this book. The thought may have crossed your mind as you flipped through its pages, wondering why you allowed yourself to buy a book that so proudly embraces its pointlessness. But deep down, you know the truth—returning it would be an even greater waste of time than reading it. Here, in excruciating detail, is a humorous breakdown of why this book will remain in your possession, refund policy or not.

Reason #1: The Embarrassment Factor

Imagine walking into a bookstore or initiating an online return and explaining to a clerk why you want your money back.

"Uh, yes, I'd like to return this book. Why? Well, because it's... pointless."

The clerk stares at you, their eyebrow raised. "Didn't the title tell you that?"

"Sure, but I thought it was a joke."

And there it is: the crushing realization that you were outwitted by a book that openly declared its lack of purpose. Do you really want to endure the judgmental smirk of a store clerk or customer service representative? No, you don't. Better to keep the book and avoid the awkward conversation altogether.

Reason #2: You've Already Read It

Most refund policies state that items must be returned in new, unused condition. But here's the problem: you've already read this book, or at least enough of it to know it wasn't what you expected (even though it clearly warned you what to expect). By reading it, you've effectively "used" it, making it ineligible for a return.

Returning a book you've read is like trying to refund a sandwich you've half-eaten. Sure, you could argue it didn't meet your expectations, but you still consumed it. At this point, the book is yours, for better or worse.

Reason #3: The Sunk Cost Fallacy

The sunk cost fallacy is a psychological phenomenon where people continue investing in something because they've already put time, money, or effort into it. You've already spent your money on this book, and returning it won't get back the time you spent reading it. Instead, you'll spend even *more* time on the return process—packing it up, printing a return label, and possibly standing in line at the post office.

At some point, you'll realize the cost of the refund isn't worth the effort. And that's when the book will quietly settle into its new home on your bookshelf, never to be mentioned again.

Reason #4: The Guilt of Buyer's Regret

Let's say you do manage to overcome the embarrassment and the effort required to initiate a return. Now comes the guilt. You chose to buy this book. No one forced you. You read the title, the description, maybe even the first few pages. You knew exactly what you were getting into, yet you still handed over your money.

Returning it feels like admitting defeat—not just to the bookstore, but to yourself. It's an acknowledgment that you let curiosity (or impulsiveness) get the better of you. And really, who wants to confront that level of self-awareness over a refund?

Reason #5: It's a Conversation Starter

Sure, the book might be pointless, but it's also unique. How many people can say they own a book that openly declares its lack of purpose? Imagine the conversations it could spark:

- *"What's that book about?"*
- *"Nothing."*
- *"Why did you buy it?"*
- *"I have no idea."*

Owning this book is like owning a piece of modern art: it doesn't need to make sense to justify its existence. In fact, its absurdity is its charm. By keeping it, you're embracing the absurd and adding a quirky artifact to your collection.

Reason #6: It's a Perfect Gift for Someone Else

If you can't justify keeping the book, why not give it away? Wrap it up as a gag gift, regift it during the holidays, or pass it along to a friend who loves unconventional reads. There's always someone who will appreciate the humor or novelty of owning a book like this.

Returning it denies you the opportunity to share the absurdity with others. And isn't that what books are for—sparking connections, even if they're based on mutual confusion?

Reason #7: You Secretly Love It

Let's be honest: you don't hate this book as much as you pretend to. Sure, it's pointless, but that's part of its charm. It's self-aware, irreverent, and unlike anything else on your shelf. It's the literary equivalent of a bad movie you can't stop watching or a snack you keep eating even though it's not that great. Deep down, you know this book has earned its place in your life, if only as a reminder to think twice before making impulse purchases.

Conclusion: The Refund You'll Never Request

Could you return this book? Technically, yes. Should you? Absolutely not. The effort, embarrassment, and existential guilt far outweigh the small amount of money you'd get back. And really, isn't the absurdity of owning a book like this worth every penny?

So, congratulations, dear reader. You've embraced the folly of this purchase, and now this book is yours forever. Wear your decision like a badge of honor—or at least like a quiet reminder that sometimes, it's better to laugh at life's absurdities than try to undo them.

Appendix B: *The Author's Shameless Self-Reflection*

I owe you, dear reader, a confession. By now, you've journeyed through the labyrinth of absurdity that is this book, and you deserve to know: *Why did I write this?* Why create something so unapologetically pointless, so blatantly devoid of purpose, and then release it into the world? The answer is both embarrassingly simple and endlessly complicated.

The Birth of an Idea That Should Have Died

It started, as many bad ideas do, as a joke. A friend and I were discussing books that seemed to exist solely to fill shelves, titles with no discernible purpose beyond being printed and sold. "I could write one of those," I said, half-joking. But the idea stuck, burrowing into my mind like a splinter.

What if I did write a book that openly embraced its own lack of purpose? What if I created something that flaunted its absurdity, challenging the very notion of why books exist? At first, I dismissed it as a fleeting whim. But as the days passed, I couldn't shake the thought. The world is full of books trying to teach, inspire, or entertain. Why not create one that intentionally does none of those things?

The Uncomfortable Joy of Writing Something Meaningless

I have to admit, writing this book was fun. Liberating, even. Without the burden of trying to teach or entertain, I was free to play with ideas, meander through pointless tangents, and embrace the absurd. Every chapter was an exercise in creative freedom, a chance to explore how far I could push the boundaries of a book's purpose.

But it wasn't all smooth sailing. There were moments of doubt, when I wondered if I was wasting my time (and yours). I questioned whether anyone would understand the joke, or worse, whether they'd think it wasn't a joke at all. But those doubts only fueled me further. The more pointless this book felt, the more determined I became to see it through.

What This Book Says About Me (and Maybe About You)

If this book reveals anything, it's that I'm deeply fascinated by the absurdity of human behavior. Why do we buy things we don't need? Why do we search for meaning in places we know we won't find it? Why do we spend time and money on things that openly declare their own futility? This book is my attempt to poke at those questions—not to answer them, but to hold them up to the light and see what happens.

But it's also a reflection of my own contradictions. I wrote this book to mock the idea of pointless consumption, yet I also wrote it to sell. I wanted to create something meaningless, but I poured hours of thought and effort into its creation. It's a paradox, much like the human condition itself.

What I Hope You Take Away (If Anything)

If this book has achieved anything, I hope it's made you laugh—or at least smirk. I hope it's made you pause, even for a moment, to think about why you bought it, why you read it, and what it says about you. And if it's done none of those things, that's okay too. After all, it never promised to be profound.

In the end, this book is exactly what it claims to be: a monument to nothingness, a celebration of the absurd, and a cheeky nod to the fact that sometimes, we all need to lighten up. Life is full of pressures to be meaningful, productive, and impactful. Maybe it's okay to embrace something that defies all of that, if only for a little while.

A Final Thought (or Lack Thereof)

So, why did I write this book? Because I could. Because I wanted to. Because the idea of creating something unapologetically pointless felt, paradoxically, like a point worth making. And if you've made it to the end of this appendix, then perhaps I've succeeded in some small, absurd way.

Thank you, dear reader, for indulging me. Thank you for your curiosity, your patience, and, most importantly, your money. After all, this book may be pointless, but at least I got something out of it. And now, so have you—whether you wanted to or not.

<u>Message from the Author:</u>

I hope you enjoyed this book, I love astrology and knew there was not a book such as this out on the shelf. I love metaphysical items as well. Please check out my other books:

-Life of Government Benefits

-My life of Hell

-My life with Hydrocephalus

-Red Sky

-World Domination:Woman's rule

-World Domination:Woman's Rule 2: The War

-Life and Banishment of Apophis: book 1

-The Kidney Friendly Diet

-The Ultimate Hemp Cookbook

-Creating a Dispensary(legally)

-Cleanliness throughout life: the importance of showering from childhood to adulthood.

-Strong Roots: The Risks of Overcoddling children

-Hemp Horoscopes: Cosmic Insights and Earthly Healing

- Celestial Hemp Navigating the Zodiac: Through the Green Cosmos

-Astrological Hemp: Aligning The Stars with Earth's Ancient Herb

-The Astrological Guide to Hemp: Stars, Signs, and Sacred Leaves

-Green Growth: Innovative Marketing Strategies for your Hemp Products and Dispensary

-Cosmic Cannabis

-Astrological Munchies

-Henry The Hemp

-Zodiacal Roots: The Astrological Soul Of Hemp

- **Green Constellations: Intersection of Hemp and Zodiac**

-Hemp in The Houses: An astrological Adventure Through The Cannabis Galaxy

-Galactic Ganja Guide

Heavenly Hemp

Zodiac Leaves

Doctor Who Astrology

Cannastrology

Stellar Satvias and Cosmic Indicas

Celestial Cannabis: A Zodiac Journey

AstroHerbology: The Sky and The Soil: Volume 1

AstroHerbology:Celestial Cannabis:Volume 2

Cosmic Cannabis Cultivation

The Starry Guide to Herbal Harmony: Volume 1

The Starry Guide to Herbal Harmony: Cannabis Universe: Volume 2

Yugioh Astrology: Astrological Guide to Deck, Duels and more

Nightmare Mansion: Echoes of The Abyss

Nightmare Mansion 2: Legacy of Shadows

Nightmare Mansion 3: Shadows of the Forgotten

Nightmare Mansion 4: Echoes of the Damned

The Life and Banishment of Apophis: Book 2

Nightmare Mansion: Halls of Despair

Healing with Herb: Cannabis and Hydrocephalus

Planetary Pot: Aligning with Astrological Herbs: Volume 1

Fast Track to Freedom: 30 Days to Financial Independence Using AI, Assets, and Agile Hustles

Cosmic Hemp Pathways

How to Become Financially Free in 30 Days: 10,000 Paths to Prosperity

Zodiacal Herbage: Astrological Insights: Volume 1

Nightmare Mansion: Whispers in the Walls

The Daleks Invade Atlantis
Henry the hemp and Hydrocephalus

10X The Kidney Friendly Diet
Cannabis Universe: Adult coloring book
Hemp Astrology: The Healing Power of the Stars
Zodiacal Herbage: Astrological Insights: Cannabis Universe: Volume 2
<u>Planetary Pot: Aligning with Astrological Herbs: Cannabis Universes: Volume 2</u>
Doctor Who Meets the Replicators and SG-1: The Ultimate Battle for Survival
Nightmare Mansion: Curse of the Blood Moon
<u>The Celestial Stoner: A Guide to the Zodiac</u>
Cosmic Pleasures: Sex Toy Astrology for Every Sign
Hydrocephalus Astrology: Navigating the Stars and Healing Waters
Lapis and the Mischievous Chocolate Bar

Celestial Positions: Sexual Astrology for Every Sign
Apophis's Shadow Work Journal: : A Journey of Self-Discovery and Healing
Kinky Cosmos: Sexual Kink Astrology for Every Sign
Digital Cosmos: The Astrological Digimon Compendium
Stellar Seeds: The Cosmic Guide to Growing with Astrology
Apophis's Daily Gratitude Journal

Cat Astrology: Feline Mysteries of the Cosmos
The Cosmic Kama Sutra: An Astrological Guide to Sexual Positions
Unleash Your Potential: A Guided Journal Powered by AI Insights
Whispers of the Enchanted Grove

Cosmic Pleasures: An Astrological Guide to Sexual Kinks

369, 12 Manifestation Journal

Whisper of the nocturne journal(blank journal for writing or drawing)

The Boogey Book

Locked In Reflection: A Chastity Journey Through Locktober

Generating Wealth Quickly:

How to Generate $100,000 in 24 Hours

Star Magic: Harness the Power of the Universe

The Flatulence Chronicles: A Fart Journal for Self-Discovery

The Doctor and The Death Moth

Seize the Day: A Personal Seizure Tracking Journal

The Ultimate Boogeyman Safari: A Journey into the Boogie World and Beyond

Whispers of Samhain: 1,000 Spells of Love, Luck, and Lunar Magic: Samhain Spell Book

Apophis's guides:

Witch's Spellbook Crafting Guide for Halloween

<u>Frost & Flame: The Enchanted Yule Grimoire of 1000 Winter Spells</u>

<u>The Ultimate Boogey Goo Guide & Spooky Activities for Halloween Fun</u>

Harmony of the Scales: A Libra's Spellcraft for Balance and Beauty

The Enchanted Advent: 36 Days of Christmas Wonders

Nightmare Mansion: The Labyrinth of Screams

Harvest of Enchantment: 1,000 Spells of Gratitude, Love, and Fortune for Thanksgiving

The Boogey Chronicles: A Journal of Nightly Encounters and Shadowy Secrets

The 12 Days of Financial Freedom: A Step-by-Step Christmas Countdown to Transform Your Finances

Sigil of the Eternal Spiral Blank Journal

A Christmas Feast: Timeless Recipes for Every Meal

Holiday Stress-Free Solutions: A Survival Guide to Thriving During the Festive Season

Yu-Gi-Oh! Holiday Gifting Mastery: The Ultimate Guide for Fans and Newcomers Alike

Holiday Harmony: A Hydrocephalus Survival Guide for the Festive Season

Celestial Craft: The Witch's Almanac for 2025 – A Cosmic Guide to Manifestations, Moons, and Mystical Events

Doctor Who: The Toymaker's Winter Wonderland

Tulsa King Unveiled: A Thrilling Guide to Stallone's Mafia Masterpiece

Pendulum Craft: A Complete Guide to Crafting and Using Personalized Divination Tools

Nightmare Mansion: Santa's Eternal Eve

Starlight Noel: A Cosmic Journey through Christmas Mysteries

The Dark Architect: Unlocking the Blueprint of Existence

Surviving the Embrace: The Ultimate Guide to Encounters with The Hugging Molly

The Enchanted Codex: Secrets of the Craft for Witches, Wiccans, and Pagans

Harvest of Gratitude: A Complete Thanksgiving Guide

Yuletide Essentials: A Complete Guide to an Authentic and Magical Christmas

Celestial Smokes: A Cosmic Guide to Cigars and Astrology

Living in Balance: A Comprehensive Survival Guide to Thriving with Diabetes Insipidus

Cosmic Symbiosis: The Venom Zodiac Chronicles

The Cursed Paw of Ambition

Cosmic Symbiosis: The Astrological Venom Journal

Celestial Wonders Unfold: A Stargazer's Guide to the Cosmos (2024-2029)

The Ultimate Black Friday Prepper's Guide: Mastering Shopping Strategies and Savings

Cosmic Sales: The Astrological Guide to Black Friday Shopping

Legends of the Corn Mother and Other Harvest Myths

Whispers of the Harvest: The Corn Mother's Journal

The Evergreen Spellbook

The Doctor Meets the Boogeyman

The White Witch of Rose Hall's SpellBook

The Gingerbread Golem's Shadow: A Study in Sweet Darkness

The Gingerbread Golem Codex: An Academic Exploration of Sweet Myths

The Gingerbread Golem Grimoire: Sweet Magicks and Spells for the Festive Witch

The Curse of the Gingerbread Golem

10-minute Christmas Crafts for kids

<u>Christmas Crisis Solutions: The Ultimate Last-Minute Survival Guide</u>

Gingerbread Golem Recipes: Holiday Treats with a Magical Twist

The Infinite Key: Unlocking Mystical Secrets of the Ages

Enchanted Yule: A Wiccan and Pagan Guide to a Magical and Memorable Season

Dinosaurs of Power: Unlocking Ancient Magick

Astro-Dinos: The Cosmic Guide to Prehistoric Wisdom

Gallifrey's Yule Logs: A Festive Doctor Who Cookbook

The Dino Grimoire: Secrets of Prehistoric Magick

The Gift They Never Knew They Needed

The Gingerbread Golem's Culinary Alchemy: Enchanting Recipes for a Sweetly Dark Feast

A Time Lord Christmas: Holiday Adventures with the Doctor

Krampusproofing Your Home: Defensive Strategies for Yule

Silent Frights: A Collection of Christmas Creepypastas to Chill Your Bones

Santa Raptor's Jolly Carnage: A Dino-Claus Christmas Tale

Prehistoric Palettes: A Dino Wicca Coloring Journey

The Christmas Wishkeeper Chronicles

The Starlight Sleigh: A Holiday Journey

Elf Secrets: The True Magic of the North Pole

Candy Cane Conjurations

Cooking with Kids: Recipes Under 20 Minutes

Doctor Who: The TARDIS Confiscation

The Anxiety First Aid Kit: Quick Tools to Calm Your Mind

Frosty Whispers: A Winter's Tale

The Infinite Key: Unlocking the Secrets to Prosperity, Resilience, and Purpose

If you want solar for your home go here: https://www.harborso-lar.live/apophisenterprises/

Get Some Tarot cards: https://www.makeplayingcards.com/sell/apophis-occult-shop

Get some shirts: https://www.bonfire.com/store/apophis-shirt-emporium/

<u>Instagrams:</u>
@apophis_enterprises,
@apophisbookemporium,
@apophisscardshop
Twitter: @apophisenterpr1
Tiktok:@apophisenterprise
Youtube: @sg1fan23477, @FiresideRetreatKingdom
Hive: @sg1fan23477
CheeLee: @SG1fan23477

Podcast: Apophis Chat Zone: https://open.spotify.com/show/
5zXbrCLEV2xzCp8ybrfHsk?si=fb4d4fdbdce44dec

Newsletter: https://apophiss-newsletter-27c897.beehiiv.com/

If you want to support me or see posts of other projects that I have come over to: **buymeacoffee.com/mpetchinskg**
I post there daily several times a day

Get your Dinowicca or Christmas themed digital products, especially Santa Raptor songs and other musics. Here: **https://sg1fan23477.gumroad.com**

Apophis Yuletide Digital has not only digital Christmas items, but it will have all things with Dinowicca as well as other Digital products.